I Love My Pet
HAMSTER

Aaron Carr

www.av2books.com

Go to **www.av2books.com**, and enter this book's unique code.

BOOK CODE

K 8 2 7 6 8 3

AV² by Weigl brings you media enhanced books that support active learning.

AV² provides enriched content that supplements and complements this book. Weigl's AV² books strive to create inspired learning and engage young minds in a total learning experience.

Your AV² Media Enhanced books come alive with...

 **Audio**
Listen to sections of the book read aloud.

 Video
Watch informative video clips.

 Embedded Weblinks
Gain additional information for research.

Try This!
Complete activities and hands-on experiments.

 Key Words
Study vocabulary, and complete a matching word activity.

Quizzes
Test your knowledge.

 Slide Show
View images and captions, and prepare a presentation.

... and much, much more!

Published by AV² by Weigl
350 5th Avenue, 59th Floor New York, NY 10118
Website: www.av2books.com www.weigl.com

Library of Congress Cataloging-in-Publication Data
Carr, Aaron.
 Hamster / Aaron Carr.
   p. cm. -- (I love my pet)
 ISBN 978-1-61690-923-9 (hardcover : alk. paper) -- ISBN 978-1-61690-569-9 (online)
 1. Hamsters as pets--Juvenile literature. I. Title.
 SF459.H3C37 2012
 636.935'6--dc23
                          2011025202

Printed in the United States of America in North Mankato, Minnesota
1 2 3 4 5 6 7 8 9 0 15 14 13 12 11

062011
WEP030611

Project Coordinator: Aaron Carr   Art Director: Terry Paulhus
Weigl acknowledges Getty Images, iStock, and Dreamstime as image suppliers for this title.

I Love My Pet

HAMSTER

CONTENTS

3

I love my pet hamster.
I take good care of him.

5

My pet hamster was a puppy.
He had no fur and could not see.

7

My pet hamster
grows fast.
He was big
after just six months.

My pet hamster has large cheeks. His cheeks can stretch to hold food.

A hamster's cheeks can stretch to its shoulders.

My pet hamster has four long teeth. These teeth never stop growing.

A hamster's front teeth grow 5 inches each year.

14

My pet hamster
sleeps all day.
He wakes up at night.

My pet hamster
only eats once a day.
I give him food every night.

Eating lettuce or tomatoes
can make hamsters sick.

My pet hamster has a cage
that needs to be cleaned
every week.
It is my job to clean his cage.

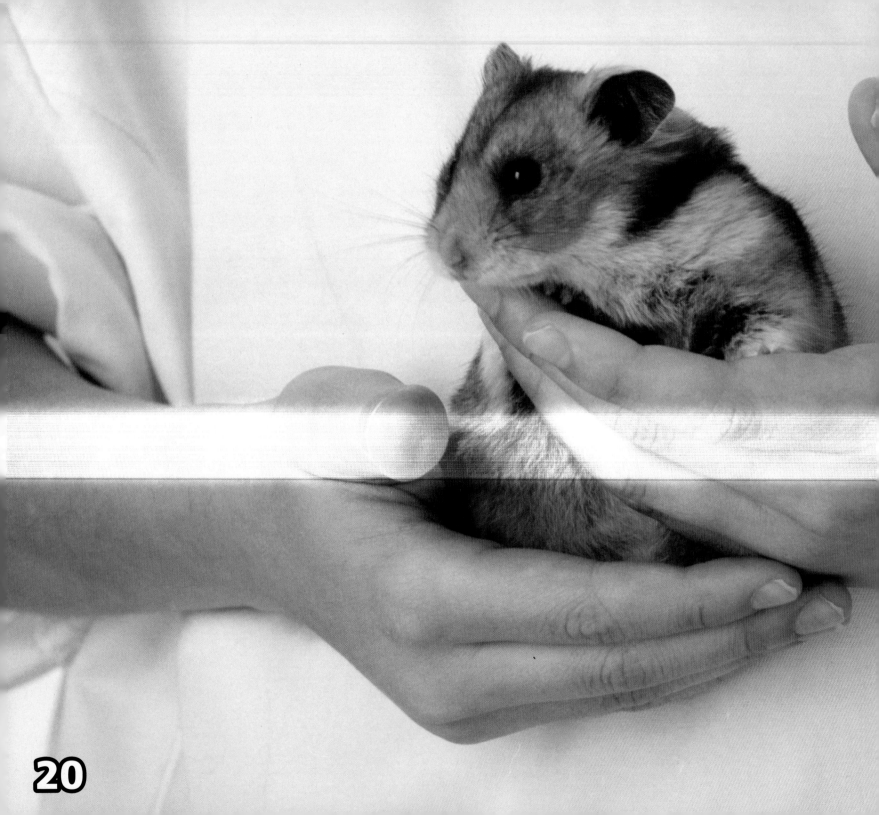

I help make sure
my pet hamster is healthy.
I love my pet hamster.

HAMSTER FACTS

This page provides more detail about the interesting facts found in the book.
Simply look for the corresponding page number to match the fact.

Pages 4–5

I love my pet hamster. I take good care of him. Hamsters are easy to care for and take up very little room. They require regular care. Hamsters need fresh food and water every day, along with comfortable shelter, grooming, and playtime. It is best to play with your hamster in the evening or night, when he is most active.

Pages 6–7

My pet hamster was a puppy. He had no fur and could not see. A baby hamster is called a puppy. Puppies are tiny and helpless at birth. Newborn puppies have no fur and cannot see or hear. Always watch puppies and their mother closely. If the mother is disturbed, feels there is not enough food, or senses danger, she may eat her puppies.

Pages 8–9

My pet hamster grows fast. He was big after just six months. By two or three weeks of age, hamster puppies are covered in soft fur and starting to eat solid foods. After five weeks, hamsters are able to live on their own. Hamsters are full grown after six months. Talk to a veterinarian to ensure your hamster receives the care it needs.

Pages 10–11

My pet hamster has large cheeks. His cheeks can stretch to hold food. Hamsters collect food and save it for later. They do this by stuffing their cheeks with food. A hamster's cheeks can stretch to the width of their shoulders. Check for rotting food when cleaning your hamster's cage. Rotten food could make your hamster sick.

Pages 12–13

My pet hamster has four long teeth. These teeth never stop growing.

A hamster's front teeth grow 5 inches each year.

My pet hamster has four long teeth. These teeth never stop growing. Hamsters have four large front teeth called incisors. A hamster's incisors grow continuously throughout its life. Hamsters have to chew constantly to file these teeth down. Make sure your hamster always has plenty of toys to chew on.

Pages 14–15

My pet hamster sleeps all day. He wakes up at night.

My pet hamster sleeps all day. He wakes up at night. Hamsters are nocturnal. This means they sleep during the day and are awake during the night. Place your hamster's cage in an area that will be quiet during the day. Hamsters can make a lot of noise at night, so keeping them in a bedroom might not be a good idea.

Pages 16–17

My pet hamster only eats once a day. I give him food every night.

Eating lettuce or tomatoes can make hamsters sick.

My pet hamster only eats once a day. I give him food every night. Hamsters should be fed once a day. It is best to feed them in the evening or night, when they are active. Hamsters need a balanced diet of grains, roots, and seeds. They also enjoy fresh fruits and vegetables, such as grapes, apples, carrots, and celery.

Pages 18–19

My pet hamster has a cage that needs to be cleaned every week. It is my job to clean his cage.

My pet hamster has a cage that needs to be cleaned every week. It is my job to clean his cage. Empty the hamster cage, but save some wood chips, bedding, and hoarded food. Clean the cage, and fill it with at least 2 inches (5 centimeters) of fresh wood chips. Finally, place the saved materials and fresh bedding in the cage.

Pages 20–21

I help make sure my pet hamster is healthy. I love my pet hamster.

I help make sure my pet hamster is healthy. I love my pet hamster. Properly fed and cared for hamsters rarely become sick. However, hamsters may become ill when they are put in stressful situations, such as too much handling or loud noises. To prevent this, keep your hamster in a quiet part of the house.

WORD LIST

Research has shown that as much as 65 percent of all written material published in English is made up of 300 words. These 300 words cannot be taught using pictures or learned by sounding them out. They must be recognized by sight. This book contains 51 common sight words to help young readers improve their reading fluency and comprehension. This book also teaches young readers several important content words, such as proper nouns. These words are paired with pictures to aid in learning and improve understanding.

Page	Sight Words First Appearance
4	good, him, I, my, of, take
6	a, and, could, had, he, no, not, see, was
9	after, big, grows, just
11	can, food, has, his, hold, large, to
12	each, four, long, never, stop, these, year
15	all, at, day, night, up
17	eats, every, give, make, once, only, or
18	be, is, it, needs, that
21	help

Page	Content Words First Appearance
4	hamster, pet
6	puppy, fur
9	months
11	cheeks, shoulders
12	inches, teeth
17	lettuce, tomatoes
18	cage, job, week

Check out av2books.com for activities, videos, audio clips, and more!

1 Go to av2books.com

2 Enter book code   K 8 2 7 6 8 3

3 Fuel your imagination online!

www.av2books.com